THE LAST DAYS OF STEAM IN
HAMPSHIRE

THE LAST DAYS OF STEAM IN HAMPSHIRE

– KEVIN ROBERTSON –

ALAN SUTTON

ALAN SUTTON PUBLISHING LTD · PHOENIX MILL · STROUD · GLOUCESTERSHIRE

First published 1987
Reprinted 1990

British Library Cataloguing in Publication Data

Last days of steam in Hampshire.
1. British Rail, *Southern Region*—
History—Pictorial works 2. Locomotives—
England—Hampshire—History—20th century—
Pictorial works
I. Robertson, Kevin
625.261094227 TJ603.4.G7

ISBN 0-86299-326-1

Endpapers: M.N. 35011 at Swaythling on up line with the Bournemouth–Waterloo Express in September 1965 – Cedric Spiller

Front Cover: 'The Southern Scene', with an original West Country Pacific at Ringwood in 1966 – From a transparency by Doug Hannah

Back Cover: An unidentified rebuilt Pacific north of Winchester on a misty morning in December 1961 – From a transparency by Doug Hannah

Typesetting and origination by
Alan Sutton Publishing Limited
Printed and bound in Great Britain by
Butler & Tanner Ltd, Frome and London

To Ian Shawyer,
thank you for helping out.

Introduction

The last years of steam in Hampshire meant more than just the passing of the steam engine. For with the introduction of the electric service to Bournemouth from 10 July 1967 steam had at last been ousted from front line duties in England. True there was still some steam in the north west but this was hardly the same as seeing a Pacific hard at work at the head of 12 coaches.

Fortunately I was able to witness at first hand those final years, although very soon after commencing work on the preparation of this book I realised that a volume containing photographs of just the period say 1963–67 would be a little restrictive. I have, therefore, adopted a wider brief covering the British Railways period in general, the theme however is still devoted to the last years.

In doing so I have been ably assisted by many good friends, and in addition have made new ones, I hope they will approve of the results. Tony Bennett, Brian Davis, John Fairman, John Fry, Graham Hawkins, Tony Molyneaux, Reg Randall, Ian Shawyer, Roger Sherlock and Roger Simmonds in particular.

Coinciding with the demise of steam was the closure of many branch lines and signal boxes, both of which are features I have tried to include in the photographs. Indeed I never realised how difficult it was preparing an album of photographs until the time came to choose the required number.

I hope then that some memories will be stirred. Of the time groups of boys would sneak into the engine sheds to collect numbers or congregate after school at a particular spot instead of perhaps doing their homework. Personally I was often in various signal boxes, no doubt trying the patience of the signalman as he attempted to explain the rudiments of block working to a youth struggling with heavy levers.

Twenty years have elapsed since steam finally disappeared, I know it is still sadly missed by many.

Kevin Robertson.

THE LAST DAYS OF STEAM IN HAMPSHIRE

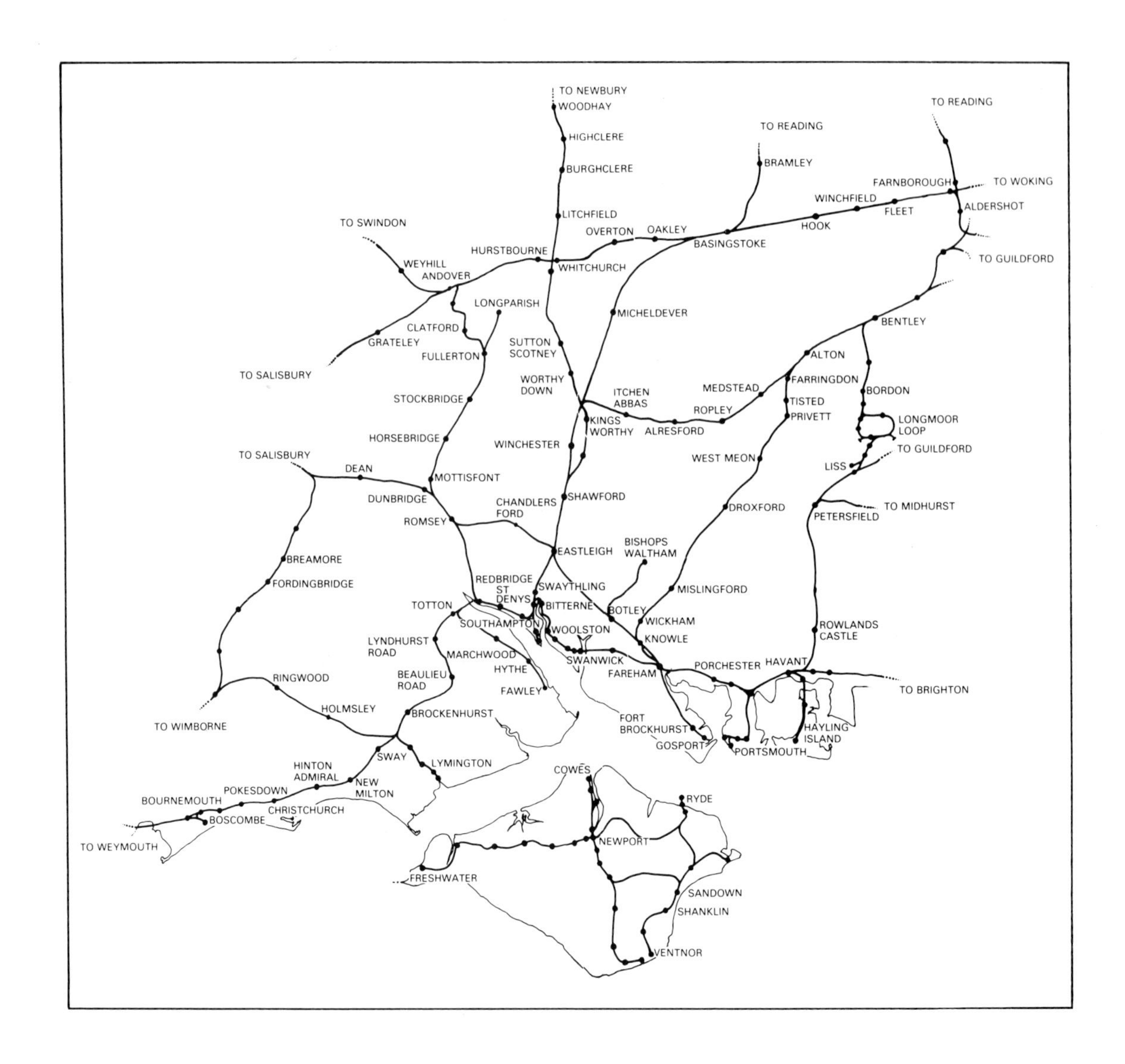

LAST DAYS OF STEAM IN HAMPSHIRE

Only locations relevant to the text are shown

At high speed 34090 *Sir Eustace Missenden* approaches Basingstoke with a non-stop from Waterloo. Waiting in the background for a path across the junction is 34042. Visit the same area today, and track rationalisation has altered the complexity of the junction to a great degree. The brash yet efficient electric sets somehow fail to create the same tingling atmosphere of a steam engine in full flight.

Collection of Brian Davis

Behind the scenes at Eastleigh running shed with the men booking on for duty.
Hugh Abbinnett

Doyen of the Merchant Navy class, 35001 *Channel Packet* at Eastleigh, nicely clean and not long out of the works. 'Merchant Navy' class engines were never allocated to Eastleigh, instead finding their way there for running in turns following overhaul or for working specials to and from Southampton Docks.

Roger Sherlock

Ready for service, the two varients of 'Bulleid Pacific' are represented here by 34002 *Salisbury* and 34025 *Whimple* outside the front of Eastleigh shed. At first glance the rebuilt 34025 shows little family resemblance to her original sister. Under British Railways the intention had been to modify the complete class of 110 engines, but the onset of modernisation precluded this and in the event 50 of the class were withdrawn still in original styling.

Roger Sherlock

The sight the travelling public saw, as 30784 *Sir Nerovans* leaves platform 2 at Eastleigh heading north under Bishopstoke road bridge. Just visible under the bridge to the left is the line to Chandlers Ford and Romsey.

E. Branch

Brightening up an otherwise grey April day in 1952, an unidentified 'Pacific' approaches Farnborough on the main line with a special working for the 'Conducted Rambles Jubilee Excursion'.

Hugh Davies

East of Basingstoke on the four track section towards Woking were several sets of automatic signals. Many were controlled by pneumatic means, recognisable by the bulbous base to each post. Passing underneath is 35026 *Lamport and Holt Line*, both steam train and signals now a matter of history.

British Railways

With the burn marks at the base of the smokebox door an indication of previous heavy working, 'D15', 30467 waits at Basingstoke in August 1955 on the 12.42 p.m. stopping service from Waterloo.

Philip Kelley

In the bay at Basingstoke where Alton bound trains would once depart, 'D15', 30465 awaits departure time with the 2.48 p.m. to Salisbury on 29.3.55. Despite being superseded by that time from front line duties, 30465 still appears presentable in overall black livery. Behind, the first coach is in the short-lived and somewhat garish 'blood and custard' colour scheme.

Philip Kelley

The 40 members of the 'Q1' class must surely have been contenders for the title the ugliest locomotives ever built. But looks apart they were certainly efficient performers, even if at times their crews had some trying moments due to their lack of really effective brakes. Nearly all their work was associated with freight traffic. 33026 entering Basingstoke down yard in April 1955.
Philip Kelley

The often forgotten, but at the time, vital side of railway operation, freight. 'S15', 30506 hurrying along the relief lines near Winchfield with a lengthy train in tow.
National Railway Museum, T.E. Williams

In an attempt to improve exhaust emmission and therefore steaming efficiency, 34064 *Fighter Command* was fitted by BR with a Giesel ejector, visible from above as an oblong chimney. The result was a great success, 'on road' performance was equal to engines of the larger 'Merchant Navy' class. The plan was then to fit several sister engines with the same equipment, but unfortunately the increasing demise of steam meant that 34064 was to remain the sole Pacific so altered by BR. She is shown here at Basingstoke after arrival from Waterloo.

D. Mackinnon

Steam and speed at Basingstoke, as 35007 *Aberdeen Commonwealth* leans into the curve through Platform 2 with a West of England express. The steam caught hanging above the top of the smokebox door was caused by a vacuum created ahead of the chimney when running fast.
D. Mackinnon

Named after the former RAF Commander, 34054 *Lord Beaverbrook* is prepared for duty at Basingstoke shed. Interestingly, the engine carries the red and white electrification warning flashes for overhead live wires, although the occasions when Southern Region machines went 'under the wires' were few and far between.

Collection of Brian Davis

During the last few months of steam operation, most of the remaining 'Pacifics' had their nameplates removed in an effort to thwart the attempts of unscrupulous souvenir hunters. Sometimes just the supports were left as with 34008, formerly *Padstow* alongside Basingstoke shed in early 1967.

John Fairman

About to start from Basingstoke bound for Waterloo on the up relief line, 'H15', 30333 has both starter and distant signals at clear. Visible to the left is the connection to Reading and the 'Western' goods yard. A considerable amount of interchange took place between the various yards.
National Railway Museum, P. Ramsome Wallis

Last days at Basingstoke with the mechanical signalling already partly dismantled and the electrified third rail ominously in place. Just leaving the station is an unidentified 'Pacific', whilst an equally grimy 34057 *Biggin Hill* starts to follow with what is probably a Salisbury bound service.
D. Mackinnon

Another 'S15' hauling freight, less glamorous perhaps, but for many years, earning more revenue than the passenger services. Entering Basingstoke on the slow line is 30843 with a Woking to Eastleigh mixed service.

E. Wilmshurst

With the fireman looking back to ensure the whole train is in tow, 30502 leaves Basingstoke up yard probably bound for Feltham.

National Railway Museum, P. Ransome Wallis

A trio of 'Standards', left to right, 73119, 73118 and 73020 at Basingstoke in September 1966.
E. Wilmshurst

At the end of the down yard at Basingstoke a single line branch turns away from the main route towards Alton. The route was closed to passengers in 1932, although a stub-section remained until as late as 1974. Passing by the point of divergence is an original 'Merchant Navy', 35011 *General Steam Navigation*. The parallel line of telegraph poles and wires another long vanished feature of the railway scene.

Philip Kelley

Just west of Basingstoke is Worting Junction and the end of the four track section from London. Here the Bournemouth and Salisbury lines diverge, a flyover junction allowing up and down trains on both routes to run simultaneously without delaying each other. 34059 *Sir Archibald Sinclair* coming off the flyover on 25.7.64 with a relief Bournemouth–Bradford service.

E. Wilmshurst

The 21 miles between Basingstoke and Winchester have only one intermediate station, Micheldever, making this the longest gap between stations anywhere from Waterloo to Bournemouth. Because of this distance passing loops were provided to facilitate working. 76014 about to rejoin the main line from the down loop with a stopping service for Eastleigh. Out of sight to the right the siding led off to an extensive goods yard and storage area, utilised in later years as an oil terminal.

Collection of R. Blencowe

Headcode discs were intended as an indicator to the signalmen as to the destination or type of train, although confusion could arise when the incorrect code was put up. This was the case here, 'S15', 30513 near Micheldever bound for Basingstoke but with discs indicating a Salisbury working.

A. Molyneaux

Devoid of name and number plates an almost immaculate 34089, heads north near Micheldever with a train of welded rail from the engineers depôt at Redbridge bound for Woking Yard. The cleanliness of the engine so late in the life of steam, March 1967, indicates that she had been prepared for a special working, and very unlikely the train shown here!

E. Wilmshurst

Just entering Winchester and with Park Road bridge in the background, 'M7' tank-engine 30250 passes the former Baltic Platform en route for Eastleigh. Crouched in the grass is Winchester enthusiast, Eric Best, this location was a favourite with several photographers.

E. Branch

Seen from the same site, 'S15', 30840 heads for Eastleigh with a mixed goods from Nine Elms. The failure of a similar train here early one summer morning was enough to cause monumental delays that lasted the whole day.

E. Branch

Winchester Junction, two miles north of the station of the same name, was once the divergence of two branches. One, out of sight behind the signalbox, leading to Alton and the second, on the left, a wartime connection to Worthy Down on the former GWR line to Newbury. After 1950 the Worthy Down connection was unused for through traffic, and instead served as a long siding for the storage of wagons and coaches awaiting works attention. Access being from the Newbury end. Big boilered 'N15', 30489 passing the severed junction with a southbound Bournemouth line service. Along with 30491, this was the last survivor of the class, operational until 1961.
Collection of R. Blencowe

Bursting back into daylight from the gloom of Wallers Ash Tunnel, 35008, one of the last active 'Merchant Navy's' heads north for Basingstoke in the summer of 1966.
Collection of M. Sumner

Freak weather conditions could also be the cause of unpunctual running. As on New Years Day 1962, when the 10.30 a.m. Waterloo–Bournemouth was one hour late passing Winchester because of frozen points and signals. 35002 *Union Castle*, slowly passing a hand signalman whilst other men attempt to remove a coating of ice from around a number of signal wires.

Peter Swift

Relaxation for the photographer perhaps but hardly for the railwaymen, as 76029 shunts the up yard at Winchester by Andover Road bridge on 1.1.62.

Peter Swift

For many years a little 'B4' dock tank-engine was the regular shunter at Winchester City, 30093 alongside Winchester Ground Frame 'A', which controlled the exit from the yard onto the up main line.

R.C. Riley

Last of the 'B4' tank-engines to work at Winchester was 30096, the crew of which posed with their engine shortly before its withdrawal in 1963. As built the cabs of these engines gave limited protection to the crews, the plating by the side windows an indication of the previous arrangement.

Hampshire Chronicle

An unusual view of Winchester City in April 1965, as 34022 *Exmoor* passes a strangely deserted goods yard. The steam escaping from underneath the cab, an indication that the fireman is attempting to get one of the injectors to function.

Collection of R. Blencowe

There were two stations at Winchester, City on the main line between Basingstoke and Southampton and Chesil on the branch from Newbury. The City station was certainly the busiest, even if this is not readily apparent here. 34109 *Sir Trafford Leigh-Mallory*, last but one of the 'Light Pacifics' leaving the main line station for Waterloo.

R.C. Riley

Winchester in panoramic form, as 34017 *Ilfracombe* enters a crowded up platform with an early morning train for Waterloo. The diesel shunter on the right having replaced the 'B4's as yard shunters.

Rod Hoyle

For the benefit of both first and second class ticket holders, an observation saloon borrowed from the Eastern Region was attached to certain Bournemouth line trains for a short while from 23.8.66. onwards, enabling 12 invited passengers to witness progress on the modernisation works. Those invited were also provided with light refreshments en route.

Hampshire Chronicle

Busy times at Winchester City as 34098 *Templecombe* heads north watched by a solitary spotter. The same wall was often crowded to capacity with boys and their notebooks. By the down platform a diesel unit waits to depart, the 'V' just visible on the end of the diesel an indication to station staff as to which end of the set the luggage compartment was situated.

A. Molyneaux

Just past St. Cross, south of Winchester, 76015 is in charge of a Waterloo–Portsmouth Harbour working, via Eastleigh. Just visible on the end of the first coach the numbers 977 can be read; the Southern forming coaches into sets, usually of either 3 or 6 vehicles, and identified by a set number. This particular rake consisting of 3 vehicles, behind which is a motley selection of older equipment.

E. Branch

Entering the 62 yard tunnel at St. Cross, 34043 *Combe Martin* at the head of a Waterloo–Bournemouth West working. The railway at this point is underneath the Winchester–Southampton road near to what is known as Bushfield roundabout.

E. Branch

Taking the place of one of the big '9F's' on a tanker train for Fawley, a green liveried 'D 6524', runs on the down relief towards Eastleigh having just come off the branch from Newbury. The two open wagons separating the engine and tank cars were a precaution then exercised whenever flamable tanks were in tow, and intended as a guard against stray sparks from a steam engine.

A. Molyneaux

The down loop from Shawford Junction as far as Shawford was a 1943 addition, the recent construction apparent in the differing shades of brickwork on the overbridge in the background. 'Q1', 33025 has just joined the loop from Winchester Chesil with a mixed train including several cattle wagons in October 1954.

J.L. Farmer

As work progressed with the extension of the third rail network towards Bournemouth, many apprehensive voices were raised as to the environmental effect a live rail would have upon wildlife. Another complaint concerned the necessary, but starkly designed sub-stations positioned at intervals along the route. This one is near Shawford, against the background of the ancient St. Catherines Hill.

Hampshire Chronicle

The 'T14' class engines were early casualties under BR, having all been scrapped by 1951. One of their last regular workings was an evening Southampton Docks–Nine Elms goods. 30461 seen working hard against the gradient as it approaches Shawford on 5.8.50. Withdrawal of these engines also meant the loss of their characteristic exhaust beat, the four cylinders producing a note totally unlike any other steam engine.

B. M. Barber

An intrusion into an otherwise serene and peaceful Ithen Valley as 35028 *Clan Line* hurries north near Otterbourne in May 1965 with a London bound express.

Rod Hoyle

Passing over the Eastleigh–Twyford Road at Allbrook, Didcot based 3211 heads for Southampton Terminus on 30.1.60.

P.J. Cupper

Previously used almost exclusively on top link duties, this is something of a come down for 'King Arthur' class 30790 *Sir Villiars* heading south on the down relief line between Shawford and Eastleigh only a few months before withdrawal.

A. Molyneaux

Having been built at Eastleigh, a train of the brand new electric stock for the Ilford–Southend service heads north near Allbrook destined for the Eastern Region on 19.2.56. The engine another 'King Arthur' relegated to menial tasks, 30768 *Sir Balin*.

Les Elsey

Returning from a derailment at Whitchurch on the Newbury branch, '700' class 30312 heads the breakdown crane and vans under Bishopstoke Road bridge Eastleigh bound for the running shed.

A. Molyneaux

Indirectly working towards its own demise, a filthy BR design 'Class 4' tank-engine with a materials train alongside the site of the new panel signal box at Eastleigh in early 1966. In the background the skyline is dominated by three structures, the church (since destroyed by fire), the building in the distance the former railway institute, (now also demolished) and the railway goods shed which still survives.

British Railways

There were four mechanical signal boxes with the name of Eastleigh, north, south, east and west, although not conforming with the expected points of the compass. Instead the South Western had adopted a practice of referring to the 'box nearest Waterloo as east and that furthest away as west, this regardless of their true geographical siting. North and south then fitted in accordingly. In what would appear to be a confusing situation, Eastleigh west box is shown here and which stood at the south end of the station! The view was taken in its last days, as already an electric ground signal and point motors await being brought into use.

John Fairman

One of the most interesting special trains of the 1950's was that of 14.6.52, which involved a tiny 'C14' tank-engine running to Bishops Waltham from Eastleigh. The first passenger train to use the branch from Botley for 19 years. Awaiting departure from platform 4, 30589 headed first towards Fareham, before running round at Botley for the short trip up the branch.

Philip Kelley

What was very nearly a major incident, as 6923 *Croxteth Hall* comes cautiously to a standstill on the up main line at Eastleigh with a wagon axle box on fire. What made the situation more dangerous were the laden tank cars behind, although fortunately the situation was dealt with rapidly.

Eric Best

Tall signals were a feature of the railways for many years, those for the up lines at Eastleigh positioned so as to be seen above the various station buildings and against a sky background. Just before their replacement in the early 1950's 'D15' 4-4-0, 30464 passes underneath the gantry with a Waterloo–Lymington train, the 'D15' engines were the regular motive power for these services.

E. Branch

Until the end of the 1950's, horses were a regular feature of the railways, used both for shunting and cartage work. Locally, horse shunting had given over to steam some years before, but up to 1952 Eastleigh retained a mare for hauling the dray used for the collection and delivery of small goods around the town. Driver and animal shown on one of their last outings before 'modernization'.

E. Branch

A Western Region visitor in the form of 6980, formally *Llanrumney Hall* at platform 3, Eastleigh with the afternoon York–Bournemouth. At this time, 1965, steam still had over two years to go on the Southern, although 6980 was withdrawn a matter of months later along with all other Western Region steam engines under full dieselisation of the W.R.

Roger Sherlock

Tearing through Eastleigh with the up Bournemouth Belle, 35029 *Ellerman Line* shatters the afternoon quiet, whilst a 'Hampshire' diesel unit waits on an Alton–Southampton Terminus train. Coupled next to the tender the full brake is painted in chocolate and cream livery, and was used exclusively with the Bournemouth Belle set. The whole train was then in pleasing uniform guise.
D. Mackinnon

The Eastleigh works shunter, 32563 slowly draws a newly overhauled 'H15', 30475 out from the works yard before setting back towards the running shed. 30475 then due to undertake a test run before returning to its home shed.

Collection of R. Blencowe

Within the usually closed confines of the works at Eastleigh, strange sights were sometimes found. Such as here in July 1963, when the withdrawn 34055 was in use as a stationary boiler and yet with the smokebox door from another condemned 'Pacific', 34043. The appearance of an engine in steam and yet minus coupling rods is hard to believe without photographic evidence.

Eric Best

Besides being the main works for the Southern Region, Eastleigh also undertook outside repairs. One of these the overhaul of Longmoor Military Railway 2-10-0, 601 *Kitchener,* which presented a decidedly foreign appearance complete with smokebox headlamp.

Eric Best

With the ever increasing frequency of steam engine withdrawals, a panel was established to decide upon certain examples which would be retained as part of a national collection. GWR, 2818 was one of those chosen and sent to Eastleigh for cosmetic overhaul ready for eventual display. The gleaming result was a tribute to the workforce. Although one may ponder for a moment on the thoughts of former Southern men given the task of working on an engine formerly operated by their arch rivals the GWR.

Roger Sherlock

Perhaps snow was forecast, as 30030 brings a local service into Eastleigh past the works offices. Spanning the track in the background is Campbell Road bridge, the only means of road access to both works and running shed and the vantage point from which countless enthusiasts have to this day stood and watched the trains go by.

Collection of R. Blencowe

Seen from the Campbell Road bridge is one of the massive '9F's', used primarily on the heavy oil trains to the Midlands. 92085 displaying a well stocked, if somewhat suspect load of coal and so is probably making for the north yard to take over a service from Fawley.

Roger Sherlock

There were three main steam sheds in Hampshire, Basingstoke, Eastleigh and Bournemouth. Eastleigh by far the largest as well as the busiest, with at times over 100 engines scattered around. Towards the last years the 'Bulleid Pacifics' were the most prolific type, a nicely clean 34063 *229 Squadron* outside the front of the shed and showing to adavantage the 'Boxpok' type of wheels fitted to these engines.

Roger Sherlock

The shed offices were located on the ground floor underneath the water tank, the two upper floors were once used as dormitories, but later as more office accomodation. Another Western region visitor is shown here, 7327 displaying evidence of being in need of a boiler wash-out judging from the stains on the cladding either side of the safety valves.

A. Molyneaux

When first seeing one of the 'Q1' engines an eminent designer is said to have asked, '. . . where does the key go to wind it up. . .?' 33023 displaying several suitable locations as it waits outside the front of the running shed.

A. Molyneaux

An essential feature of the depôt, the 'privvy' at Eastleigh running shed.

A. E. Bennett

Photography inside the shed was always difficult, primarily due to the contrasting patterns of light and shade. Here though the scene is portrayed to advantage as a variety of engines quietly await their next turn of duty one Sunday morning in December 1953.

Les Elsey

Austere yet functional, the front end of a 'Standard' Class 5, several members of which were allocated to the Southern from 1951 onwards. Unfortunately, these engines were hardly given the opportunity to fulfill expectations as the onset of modernisation meant many were consigned to the scrap heap despite having years of useful life remaining. 73170 of approximately equal power to the diesel behind, yet destined to be withdrawn after only about 15 years use.

A. Molyneaux

During 1947 the Southern Railway converted several engines to oil burning, an unhappy episode brought to a premature end by the inadaquacies of government. Reminders of the scheme were around for some time afterwards and included this line up of stored engines at the back of the running shed in November 1948.

Collection of John Fairman

It was a feature of the steam era that certain engines had a particuarly long life, whilst others disappeared relatively quickly. Generally those employed on shunting and goods had the longest lives, 30325 of the '700' class built to a design dating back to 1897 and shown here in overall black livery 60 years later.

M. Sumner

Photo – Les Elsey

Up Boat

A fine summers day in late July and the high cloud has little effect on a bright blue sky. The blackened gabled ends and smokeshutes of Eastleigh running shed point up towards the blueness, whilst outside slowly simmering amidst the heat haze is 30857 awaiting its next turn of duty.

The engine has already been prepared by a gang of cleaners, each dressed in overalls of pale blue liberally stained with oil and paraffin. Each of these artisans of the oily cloth has wiped and rubbed his allocated bit of engine and tender until the morning sun is reflected in the brightly gleaming metal and green paintwork.

Shortly the bright almost garish headboard *'Cunarder'* will be affixed to the smokebox indicating this is the engine destined to work the boat train from the liner *'Queen Mary'* from Southampton Docks to Waterloo.

Departure time from Southampton is not until 1.30 p.m. so when driver and fireman book on there is plenty of time to read the official notices before collecting their kit and making their way over to the engine.

Around 11.30 a.m. the crew emerge from the comparative coolness of the shed and slowly make their way over to the engine. A wisp of steam from one corner of the firebox is instantly recognisable as a leaking stay, but is insufficient to cause concern.

Climbing on board the men stow their respective 'traps' in the lockers provided. The driver having a 'Gladstone Bag' complete with a former spirit bottle of cold tea, whilst his fireman has a old gas mask case with one of the newer white stove enamel tea cans. With some time still before booked departure time the men busy themselves in preparing their engine and checking oil filler cups and sandboxes before the fireman sluices off the footplate in preparation for departure.

As the time approaches 12.35 p.m. the handle is wound into forward gear, tender handbrake released and regulator and cylinder cocks opened, and so with a ear piercing cresendo *Lord Howe* slowly moves forward. The excessive pitch only lasts a few moments for with the driver satisfied that all condensation has been expelled from the cylinders, the cocks are closed and a relative peace descends again. No doubt to the relief of those living in nearby Campbell Road whose houses back directly onto the running shed.

Slowly the engine passes under Campbell Road bridge as some of the men from the nearby works pass overhead, paying little heed to what was then an everyday sight.

The engine stops by the ground signal protecting the exit from the shed and the fireman descends to operate the train describer. This is a pale blue faced instrument analogous to a clock and consisting of a number of discs each inscribed with a particular route. The appropriate one is selected and a handle is then pushed in the indication being repeated in the nearby signal box so that the signalman can route each departing engine onto its correct line. This time it is 'Down Main Line' that is selected and so with the ground signal 'off', 30857 slowly trundles onto the main line before reversing to gain the direction of the docks.

HUGH ABBINNETT

Having worked its last duty and still with its Southern Railway number, Adams' design X6, 440 of 1895 stands awaiting its fate on the scrap road of the shed.

Trevor Rowe

A sad end for USA tank-engines 'DS235' and 'DS236' at the back of the works in August 1965. As with many works, Eastleigh cut up a number of steam engines themselves, with others dealt with at the running shed. But as the pace of withdrawals quickened the railway's own resources were inadaquate and so engines were sold to outside scrap dealers in various parts of the country.

Roger Sherlock

An often forgotten, but essential feature of any running shed was the supply of coal and removal of ashes. 80013 performing the latter task at Eastleigh at the head of 9 mineral opens, the last of which is receiving its quota of clinkers. After the train has been reformed the engine will pull it around the triangle at the back of the works preparatory to transfer to the marshalling yards and eventual routing for dumping.

Roger Sherlock

Minus its smokebox plate, but still retaining a nameplate, 73086 *The Green Knight* outside the shed. These engines were sometimes preferred by the Eastleigh men to a 'Pacific', having the advantage of reliability in performance compared with the often eccentric behaviour of the original 'Bulleid' design. Against this though were the drafty cabs, whilst a Pacific on a good day was probably without equal anywhere in the country.

Roger Sherlock

Another visitor in the form of LMS design '8F', 48724 posed between duties. The Southern never owned any 8-coupled tender engines and consequently the heavy inter-regional freights of the 1950's and early 60's brought several types of LMS and GWR engine to Hampshire. In addition Eastleigh also conducted overhauls on some members of the class, 48724 apparently not long out of works judging by the gleaming paintwork for what was a freight engine.

Roger Sherlock

The 'Z' class tank-engines were infrequent visitors to Hampshire, spending most of their lives shunting either in the London area or on banking duties at Exeter. However, there is always an exception as 30952 was for many years the Eastleigh north yard shunter, although it is depicted here as withdrawn and awaiting the cutters torch. The view also shows the standard practice of tying up the motion of a condemmed engine with rope, whilst one of the coupling rods is also secured to the top of the side tank and seen poking through the cab spectacle.

Roger Sherlock

The period from about 1962 onwards saw an ever increasing influx of visiting engines, some on special workings and others not. Eastleigh still primarily a steam 'hotspot' and so able to cope with tasks other workshops were turning away due to their own modernisation programmes. An example of this is the London Midland 2-6-0, 43019 at the back of the shed, waiting to return to home after a 'sole and heel' repair.

Roger Sherlock

Totally unlike any other steam design on the Southern were the 14 USA tank-engines, purchased in 1946 from the U.S. Army for dock shunting. Some members of the class lasting right up to the end of steam in July 1967, a rather grimy 30071 acting as the Eastleigh shed pilot in 1965 whilst the crew give their own version of the 'Royal Wave'.

Roger Sherlock

Yet another visitor and also in unusual livery. 'L94', a former GWR pannier tank sold out of service to London Transport and based at their Neasden depot. The engine was at Eastleigh for repair and sporting an unofficial crest from its former owners on the bunker side.

Roger Sherlock

Despite the fact that snow is a relatively rare occurance near the south coast, it was common practice to prepare an engine for snow plough duties from early December onwards. On this occasion 'Q' class 0-6-0, 30535 had the task, the plough a semi-permanent addition, as for the duration of the time it was carried the front buffers were also removed.

Roger Sherlock

Signal details of the down starter at Swaythling in 1965.

John Fairman

St. Denys was also the junction for the Netley and Fareham line, 30467 passing under a fine array of lower quadrant signals as it takes the route to Fareham. The station had four platform faces, those on the left only accesible to main line trains, whilst those on the right were similarly for Netley line trains only.

Collection of R. Blencowe

In common with Southampton Terminus, the maze of lines at Northam is now just a memory, those on the right, including the scissors crossover, providing access to the Chapel Tramway. 'T9', 30707 shown heading south in November 1960 near to Chapel Level Crossing en route to Southampton Terminus with a mixed van train.

P.J. Cupper

The 16.6.58 saw superpower for a Waterloo–Bournemouth stopping service with *Lord Nelson* 30853, *Sir Richard Grenville* leaving St. Denys with a trailing load of only four coaches.

A. Molyneaux

South of Eastleigh the main line runs parallel to Southampton Airport and past the diminutive signal box and cottage at Stoneham. 7928, *Wolf Hall* heading for Bournemouth on an excursion from Kidderminster in April 1960.

A. Molyneaux

A regular feature of interest at Southampton was Chapel Tramway, a small industrial concern connecting the various wharfs with the BR network at Northam. Seen by many, it was little photographed although here the camera has caught a Peckett 0-4-0 crossing Marine Parade with a train for the interchange sidings.

Eric Best

At Northam Junction the Bournemouth line parts company from the original route to Southampton, the new line taking a sharp curve to pass under the Southampton–Portsmouth road before entering Southampton Tunnel. Rounding the curve northwards is 30782 *Sir Brian*, in charge of the Bournemouth–Birkenhead through train in the summer of 1951.

Les Elsey

34010, *Sidmouth* at the head of the down 'Cunarder' passing Southampton Terminus and nearly at jouneys end. Compared with the earlier view the headboard can be seen to be considerably different, whilst another variation for the same train involved a ships funnel in the characteristic red and black of the steamship company.

Les Elsey

All appears hustle and bustle at Southampton Terminus, yet less than a decade later almost all was swept away to leave a desolate wasteland. In happier times 75006 backs out from the lines leading to the Docks and heads for Northam and perhaps Eastleigh. The tender at least showing signs that replenishment is perhaps required.

R. Sherlock

Here the connections into the docks show up well on the left, one of the dock shunters waiting by the signal whilst another busies itself alongside. The 'T9' leaving under a clear signal for Eastleigh with empty stock.

National Railway Museum, P. Ransome Wallis

Most of the prestige boat-trains commenced or terminated their journey at the Southampton Ocean Terminal. A massive concrete and glass edifice erected in a somewhat garish style in the early 1950's. Somehow steam trains and the building seemed to go well together as here with 34090, now bereft of nameplates awaiting its compliment of passengers. The three luggage vans immediately next to the tender an indication as to the amount of luggage the liner passengers would carry.

Roger Sherlock

Before the advent of the standard 40ft. containers of today, smaller individual units were utilised for local movement of goods. The railway advertising a 'door-to-door' service although unfortunately, the flexibility of the road vehicle meant an end to this type of traffic. Eastleigh based 'Class 4' tank-engine, 80152 preparing to leave the old (Eastern) docks with one of the last steam hauled freights including containers of meat.

Roger Sherlock

Connecting the Terminus Station with the Docks was a level crossing over the busy Canute Road. 70004, *William Shakespeare* one of the two 'Britannia Pacifics' at one time time allocated to the Southern cautiously crossing the road. Britannia Pacifics were officially banned from the docks, and rightly so, for 70004 derailed herself on the sharp curves in the docks later that day. The visit was apparantly made without official authority.

Les Elsey

Steam engines continued to run into the Docks right up to the end of steam. April 1967 for example finding 34036 crossing an unusually quiet Canute Road with a special boat train. In the background is the massive South Western Hotel, named after the railway company that built it and intended to attract the patronage of the affluent transatlantic passengers.

E. Wilmshurst

Within the docks numerous access roads criss-crossed the railway lines, each of which was invariably busy during the day and so any movement of trains had to be carefully controlled. 30860, *Lord Hawke* seeming somewhat out of place amidst the cars, tarmac and trees.
Roger Sherlock

Off the main line it was possible to find all manner of ancient machines. A diminutive 'C14', 0-4-0, No. 77s at work near Southampton Town Quay just before Christmas 1957. The Town Quay sidings were accesible off part of the connecting link between the Old and New Docks.

A. Molyneaux

Linking the Terminus and Central Stations at Southampton was a sharp curve deviating off the main Bournemouth line at Tunnel Junction. As the name implies this was very close to the tunnel leading to Southampton Central Station. Controlling the junction, as well as the main line either side, was a tall and very old signal box, the signalman was able to observe movement over the whole area from his lofty perch. 34109, *Sir Trafford Leigh-Mallory,* just passing the 'box and entering onto the sharp curve leading to Northam Junction with the 11.16 a.m. Bournemouth West–York train. Ironically the connection to the Terminus was electrified at the same time as the main line, although electric services never ran over it. The connection and box were removed by 1973.

Pamlin Prints

The connection between the Old and New docks ran for part of its course alongside a busy road, the sharp curves and check rails associated with the route showing up well. Nearing the Town Quay is USA tank-engine 30062 at the head of an 'RCTS' special. The railway at this point, steam engine and motor cars are now all part of history.

W. Gilburt

Inside Tunnel Junction 'box with the lever frame unusually positioned at 90° to the main line. The block shelf above the brightly polished levers presenting an array of 'lock & block' equipment now highly prized by collectors.

A. Molyneaux

Against a background of the Southampton Civic Centre Clock Tower, 34047, *Callington* brings the 11.00 a.m. Brighton–Cardiff service into 'Central Station on 8.8.53. The train later running via Romsey to Salisbury where an engine change took place.

Philip Kelley

The Tunnel at Southampton passes right under the very heart of the City, its path through a quantity of unstable ground meaning maintainance costs have always been high. On 4.7.67 with less than a week to go before the cessation of steam working, 34095, by then unnamed, leads the Poole–Birmingham train into the cavernous interior, and the last time this particular train was steam worked.

D. Mackinnon

Underneath the well known signal gantry at the west end of Southampton Central, 34040, *Crewkerne* clearly displays the filth inseperable from the steam engine in its final years. At first glance the oil lamps of the signals appear to stand out well, but against the electric lamps of the roadside there is little comparison.

D. Mackinnon

The inconvenience of the train, 35023 *Holland Afrika Line* watched by postmen crossing the line at Southampton in June 1965.

Rod Hoyle

Behind the scenes in the ticket office with an almost limitless variety of little pieces of cardboard to most destinations in the country.

Collection of Graham Hawkins

Despite its importance there was rarely a pilot engine on duty at Southampton, any shunting usually undertaken by the engine from the various local services that arrived or terminated at the station. 'M7', 30479 leaving the bay platform at the west end of the station for Fawley whilst an unidentified 'King Arthur' runs in from Bournemouth.

Collection of I. Shawyer

Another view of 35023 in grimy condition, pausing by platform 1, Southampton Central and attracting the attention of a young admirer. Ominously conductor rails are positioned in the 'four-foot' waiting to be laid, the puddle on the middle platform presumably from the water column!

Roger Sherlock

Class 4 tender engine, 76017 passing the signal box at 'Central on what is believed to be a Portsmouth bound working, the board hanging from the top lamp bracket an indication of the crew duty number. Inside 'Central box two men and a booking boy will be on duty, the interior maintained in spotless condition with a floor clean enough to eat off.

W. Gilburt

34012, *Launceston* makes a spirited start from Southampton westwards, its apparant sure-footedness not always a regular feature of the 'Bulleid Pacifics'. Above the name plate is the coat of arms of the town of Launceston, whilst underneath a small brass scroll proclaims 'West Country Class'.

Roger Sherlock

Problems just west of Southampton Central, when an electrical fault caused a set of points to move just as a train was approaching. Fortunately no one was injured although the disruption to services was considerable. By the time this view was taken some of the stock had been cleared away although the Eastleigh breakdown gang is in attendance clearing the derailed coaches. 30316 ready to draw the vehicles clear as soon as they are re-railed.

A. Molyneaux

Non-stop through Millbrook, a pair of 'M7's' working a Southampton–Fawley service. Despite the use of the two engines speed would be unlikely to be much above 35 m.p.h., the riding qualities of the elderly stock somewhat uncomfortable above those speeds.

W. Gilburt

Almost the end, with conductor rail laid and concrete troughing for colour light signal wiring alongside. 73117 passing Lyndhurst Road signal box and a somewhat drunken telegraph pole whilst working the 9.33 a.m. Waterloo–Bournemouth service.

E. Wilmshurst

In finest railway tradition, Lyndhurst Road station was some miles away from the location of the same name. Indeed Ashurst would have been far more suitable. Seen from the Southampton end the layout displays the typical characteristics of a wayside stopping place, even the goods yard full to capacity, although the station-masters greenhouse was not always a regular feature.

British Railways

Approximately mid-way between Southampton and Bournemouth comes Brockenhurst, situated in the midst of the lucious New Forest. Here there was a commodious station with bays either side, its importance reflected in the junctions a little further west for Lymington and Ringwood. The Lymington branch was steam hauled almost to July 1967, gaining the melancholy distinction of being the last steam branch anywhere in the country. 80134 waiting in the up bay at Brockenhurst before running round to return to Lymington.

John Rooney

A feature of the railways in the days of steam were the number of through workings now long since disappeared. One of these was from Brighton to Bournemouth, 'L' class 4-4-0, 31778 at Brockenhurst whilst working the train on 3.1.59.

E. Wilmshurst

Freight trains even in the Forest were a common sight, the yard at Brockenhurst often busy for much of the day. There were also a number of westbound goods services, one of these having just left Brockenhurst on 14.10.61 with 31619 in charge.

A. Molyneaux

Lymington Junction just west of Bournemouth and with 34045, *Ottery St. Mary* leaving the old route to the west via Ringwood with a local Bournemouth West–Brockenhurst stopper. The Ringwood line was also used as a diversion whenever the new line via Sway was out of use, although its curved path precluded any attempt at high speed running.

E. Wilmshurst

Seen on the opposite side, 'Q' class 0-6-0, 30542 joins the main line with a train from Lymington, the fireman having just placed the tablet for the single line on the catcher just ahead of the signal.

T. Rowe

Viewed across the harbour bridge at the entrance to Lymington Marina, 80152 heads a Brockenhurst train close by the Town station.

E. Wilmshurst

Another often forgotten aspect of railway traffic was that of pigeon trains. Baskets of often valuable birds sent to various destinations for release at a pre-determined time. 33020 running back towards the main line from Lymington with a now empty pigeon special in August 1953.
R.C. Riley

Major engineering work between Sway and New Milton in early 1948 necessitated single line working controlled from various temporary signal boxes. The 'Bournemouth Belle' cautiously passing the short lived Hordle 'box whilst 'blanketing' of the formation takes place. Travel on the 'Belle was by Pullman car only, a supplement payable on top of the standard first class fare. For this meals were available served at every seat although again at extra cost. The train making one trip each way daily from Waterloo to Bournemouth until withdrawn at the time of electrification.
British Railways

Engineering work again, but this at Christchurch just east of Bournemouth. The white stakes driven into the ballast an indication as to how far the necessary slewing of track must take place. Christchurch was once a terminus station on a short branch from Ringwood, this later extended to reach Bournemouth along the course of the present line with the original branch long since closed.

British Railways

On 19.8.64, Oxford Shed provided 6917, *Oldlands Hall* for the York–Bournemouth train, seen passing the Pickfords depository at Christchurch and nearing journeys end.

Roger Sherlock

The approach to Bournemouth Central Station was via a skew bridge under Holdenhurst Road. The slow speed of trains entering the station giving the impression of a tunnel rather than just a bridge. 34086, *219 Squadron* arriving at the platform with another inter-regional service, the 8.30 a.m. from Newcastle-on-Tyne in July 1965.

E. Wilmshurst

Prior to local government re-organisation and the consequent adjustment of county boundaries, Bournemouth was within the county of Hampshire. This remained so throughout the life of the steam engine in the county. As depicted previously the station was also a favourite with the enthusiast, the long down platform providing an excellent vantage point from which to view the comings and goings at the engine shed opposite. 76019 blocking the view temporarily as it stands on pilot duty in early 1964.

Roger Sherlock

Spotters sometimes argue for hours over the relative merits or failings of various types of locomotive. Conversation ceasing at least temporarily as two youthful enthusiasts seek to identify an ex-Great Western 'Hall' as it arrives at Bournemouth in June 1965. The short hair cuts I am sure bringing back memories to many.

Rod Hoyle

Replenishing the tender, June 1965.

Rod Hoyle

Withdrawal of the 'Bulleid Pacifics' commenced in 1962. 34030, *Watersmeet* an early casualty. In happier times the engine is seen reversing off the turntable at Bournemouth and past the well known sign 'Quiet Please, Residential Area'.

Collection of Ian Shawyer

The very last day of steam working, 9.7.67, and with Bournemouth shed host to an unidentified 'Standard' sandwiched between more modern types of motive power.

A. E. Bennett

After the withdrawal of both passenger and through freight services from the D.N. & S. line a thrice weekly freight working continued to run until early 1966. One of these trains leaving Bar End Yard at Winchester Chesil bound for Eastleigh behind 2-6-4 tank-engine, 80015.
Rod Hoyle

Moving off the main line now to a quieter backwater, the former Newbury line from Shawford Junction. Eastleigh crews would sometimes refer to the branch as a 'trip off the timetable and onto the calender', a somewhat unkind reference to the leisurely schedules applying to this route. Having not long joined the branch from the main line, 92231 passes by Garnier Road, Winchester and the car park by the River Itchen. The engine driver looking as if he would willingly change places with some of the walkers, whilst to them the train hardly warrents a second glance.
Peter Swift

During 1963 in connection with the centenary of King Alfreds College Winchester, a special train was run to Winchester Chesil with the passengers dressed in contemporary costume. Motive power was provided in the form of the then restored 'T9', 120. The brightly coloured engine in stark contrast to the dismal station building, recently deprived of its canopy and footbridge.
E.A. Sollars

Work in progress on dismantling the canopy at Winchester Chesil, as an unknown Standard Class 4 hurries south towards Eastleigh past the watchful gaze of porter 'Topper' Brown.
Hampshire Chronicle

Early in May 1964 a derailment at Reading West resulted in the Pines Express being diverted via the D.N. & S. route to Newbury and Didcot. Passengers waiting at Winchester City Station ferried to 'Chesil by a special bus. Ironically this was perhaps the longest and heaviest passenger train ever to use the branch whilst unknown at the time it was also the last passenger train to traverse its full length. 34105, *Swanage* just entering 'Chesil station and seemingly with steam to spare.
Hampshire Chronicle

Arguably a waste of resources, as contractors set out cutting up the rails on the now abandoned line to Newbury. Whilst one cannot argue on purely financial terms as to the retention of every railway route, it does appear to be a lost opportunity when a perfectly adaquate route is abandoned in favour of a road requiring countless millions to be spent on improvements.
Hampshire Chronicle

By 1959 regional boundary changes had resulted in the whole of Hampshire coming under Southern Region control, although this did not prevent 'foreign engines' appearing on through workings. Most of the time this occurred on lines formerly under Western Region control and included the Newbury route. Collett design 0-6-0, 2240 passing Winnall on a Didcot–Southampton working during the long hot summer of 1959.

Hampshire Chronicle

In 1957 the record breaking Great Western 4-4-0, *City of Truro* had a daily working over the D. N. & S. from Didcot to Southampton. The engine seen surmounting the brief climb out of Sutton Scotney station heading south for Worthy Down and Winchester.

G. Siviour

With few passengers and consequently small amounts of revenue, there was little available finance to spend on maintainance. 7327 and Sutton Scotney station unfortunately typical of much of the railway system in the late 1950's with engines in run down condition and drab passenger facilities.

Hampshire Chronicle

Conversation time at Sutton Scotney, the signalman holding the token and catcher for the previous section from Worthy Down as a Didcot train waits to leave northwards two weeks before passenger services were withdrawn in March 1960.

P.J. Cupper

Being primarily an agricultural county, the course of several railways took them through open terrain. The Newbury line a typical example of this as the 12.25 p.m. Newbury–Winchester train nears Whitchurch on 6.2.60.

E. Wilmshurst

Near Whitchurch, D.N. & S. route, 1965.

John Fairman

Rationalisation of certain of the underused facitilites on the D. N. & S. started as early as 1950. The passing loop and one of the platfroms at Litchfield taken out of use in 1955. 75005 waiting at the station on the last day of service, 5.3.60.

T. Wright

Nestling deep in the heart of rural Hampshire, the charm of Highclere station is in stark contrast to the bustle of the main line. A journey then on a branch line or secondary route was often noted for its leisurely pace and serenity. The Winchester–Newbury line was no exception to this, 30283 at the head of a light three coach load alongside what in some ways hardly resembles a railway station.

G. Siviour

On the line to Newbury the boundary with Berkshire was just near Woodhay Station, coincidentally also the last station before Newbury. Seen from the signalbox on a very wet January day in 1960, 31803 brings a long train of empties from Eastleigh bound for Didcot, the fireman leaning out ready to give up the single line token.

E. Wilmshurst

Without doubt the most controversial steam engine design of later years was Bulleids' ill fated *Leader*, which first ran in May 1949. The whole project was beset with difficulties yet makes a fascinating story of one man's attempt to prove the steam engine was still capable of further development. Suffice it to say that by early 1950, 36001 had graduated to Eastleigh from where trials continued for several months. One of these is shown here with the engine at the head of an empty test train leaving Eastleigh yard for Fratton.

S.C. Townroe

Running at high speed, one estimate of this in excess of 80 m.p.h., 76014 leaves Tapnage Tunnel near Fareham on a test run from Eastleigh.

W. Gilburt

Coming off the Netley line at Fareham, B.R. 'Standard' Class 3 tank-engine, 82014 at the head of a Portsmouth bound service. The lines on the right those for Eastleigh as well as the Meon Valley.

National Railway Museum, P. Ransome Wallis

In connection with engineering works on the Bournemouth line it was common practice to divert main line trains either via Fareham or Alton. In both cases however with substantial increases in journey times. Leaving Fareham for Southampton on 28.10.62 is 73116 at the head of a Weymouth bound working. The use of Midland coaching stock was somewhat unusual at the time.
W. Gilburt

The more usual steam services at Fareham were either the through Cardiff–Brighton trains or local services. One of the latter shown here with 'T9', 30729, leaving the north end of the station with the route set for the tunnel avoiding line and Eastleigh.
W. Gilburt

The concept of the diesel train with its driver always at the front end is thought by some to be a relatively new concept. But this is certainly not the case for steam-railcars on the same principle were in existence very early on. Another variation was the auto- or motor-train in which the driver operated the controls of the engine from a specially equipped coach, the fireman remaining on the footplate. A ex-South western 'motor-train' shown leaving Fareham for Portsmouth with a special working in the early 1950's.

W. Gilburt

At the south end of Fareham station the railway forked with the original line continuing straight ahead to Gosport. On the left is the later connection to Portsmouth, its legacy in the form of a sharp curve and consequent speed restriction still an operating difficulty today. An unidentified 'T9' cautiously negotiating the curve with a Portsmouth–Salisbury train.
D. Callender

The through Brighton–Eastleigh workings often resulted in a variety of motive power sometimes destined for the works and repair. Both 'Ashford' and 'Brighton' engines then performing regular duties on the services passing Fareham. Heading back in the direction of home territory 'L'class 4-4-0, 31776 has the road set for Portsmouth as it prepares to leave the station in June 1952.
Derek Clayton

Bound for Eastleigh from Lancing Carriage Works on 26.6.65, departmental shunter, DS235 developed a hot axle box at Fareham and had to shunted at Fareham for attention before continuing the last few miles of the journey. Such a failure was often enough to condem an engine in the last days of steam working and contributed to a shortage of serviceable steam motive power during the period 1965–1967.

E. Wilmshurst

Passenger services to Gosport ceased as early as 1953, although a run down of services in the area had commenced many years earlier with the closure of the Stokes Bay service as long ago as 1914. In the final years at Gosport two coaches were enough to fulfill demand, 30051 leaving the station bound for the Meon Valley route and Alton.

E.E. Smith

Gosport was visited by a number of specials in the 1960's, one shown in charge of 31411 complete with white painted buffers – they would not stay like that long! Behind the train the overall roof was erected as recently as 1950, replacing a wooden train shed unfortunately destroyed by bombing.

R. Sherlock

Beyond Gosport a short extension ran to the Royal Naval Victualling Yard, complete with two level crossings in a matter of yards. Passing over the first of these at Mumby Road, 'N' class Mogul, 31413 heads back towards Gosport after shunting Clarance Yard in May 1962.

D. Fereday Glenn

Despite having a sizeable steam shed at Fratton, steam was never as common at Portsmouth compared with its neighbour Southampton. This was simply due to the fact that the lines to Portsmouth from London and Brighton had been electrified by 1937. Even so certain workings would guarantee steam haulage, one of the these the 9.03 a.m. to Plymouth, seen awaiting departure from Portsmouth & Southsea Terminus on 11.7.64. Just visible to the left and on a higher level, are the platforms for the connection leading to Portsmouth Harbour station.

E. Wilmshurst

Following closure of the Hayling branch it was hoped the service could be maintained using more economical methods of operating. A tram service was suggested as a means of achieving this. Matters progressed as far as bringing a Blackpool Tram to Havant for assesment, but regretfully nothing more was heard of the project.

E. Wilmshurst

Compared with the large running sheds, conditions at Havant for servicing steam engines were decidedly primitive, although to be fair it was only the 'A1X' class working the Hayling Island branch that were dealt with here. At the end of the branch platform, 32661 takes on more than its fair share of water, the fireman obviously having done this before as he stands on top of the wall in an effort to keep his feet dry.

Collection of Brian Davis

The achilles heel of the Hayling branch was without doubt the wooden trestle viaduct over Langstone Harbour. Its light construction severely limiting the weight of engines able to cross, as well as being the subject of a 20 m.p.h. speed limit. This was the reason for the retention of the diminutive 'Terrier' tank-engines to operate the service. 32661 crossing the bridge at the head of a two coach train and showing to advantage the spindly bridge construction.

Collection of Brian Davis

Because of their small size, coal capacity of the 'Terrier' tank-engines was limited. A spell at the coal stage at the Hayling Island terminus was often necessary after every trip, especially with the peak season heavy trains. Coaling was also always performed by hand, which, judging from the size of some of the lumps, was likely to be a strenouous task.

Philip Kelley

Another diverted service, this time a Southampton Docks–Waterloo boat train, running over the electrified line at Bedhampton en route for Petersfield and Guildford with the more usual route regained at Woking. 34021 at the head of some eleven bogie vehicles.

E. Wilmshurst

The Portsmouth direct line via Petersfield was an early candidate for electrification, one of the principle considerations were the long hard gradients which severely taxed many an engine. Steam though continued to run on it to the end, 73115 at the head of the 9.33 a.m. Portsmouth–Surbiton parcels near Petersfield in December 1965.

E. Wilmshurst

The layout at Petersfield was unusual in that it was in effect two stations seperated by a busy level crossing; that on the north side used by Midhurst branch trains. By the early 1950's traffic on the lesser route had diminished to such an extent that one coach was all that was required, 'M7', 30108 seen with its light load just one week before final closure in February 1955.

Philip Kelley

'Poor Staff Accomodation' was the reason for recording the interior of the messing hut in Petersfield goods yard. Unfortunately, these basic facilities were by no means unique to this one location and with little money available for a rapid improvement to resources, such conditions were to plague the railways until comparatively recent times.

British Railways

At Liss, north of Petersfield a connection led off to the Longmoor Military Railway, this army system also accessible from the Borden Branch. At Longmoor itself, an extensive railway network was primarily used for training purposes and in its last years mainly operated by 'Austerity' 0-6-0 tank-engines such as Nos. 195 and 157 posed outside the Longmoor engine shed.
E. Wilmshurst

Amongst the exercises carried out on the Longmoor line were those involving derailments. An old engine deliberately derailed as practice. Unfortunately, however, genuine incidents sometimes occured, when for instance, a former GWR 'Dean Goods' collided at speed with a stationary train.
Lens of Sutton

Variety on the Southampton–Fareham line, B.R. 'Standard Class' 4, 76006 at the head of some mixed Western Region stock just entering Swanwick. This particular line was another renowned for its heavy gradients, the rails visibly disappearing behind the last vehicle, whilst a sucession of sharp curves precluded fast running.

W. Gilburt

The 10.8.57 saw 76009 passing Bursledon and the lower reaches of the River Hamble whilst on a Portsmouth to Cardiff service. The train having just crossed over the viaduct in the background on its way from Fareham.

E. Wilmshurst

On the eastern outskirts of Southampton is Bitterne Station, which despite being only two miles or so in a straight line from the centre of Southampton, by rail the distance was more than double this. Regretfully, commuter traffic has always been small. An unidentified 'Standard' rushing through the deserted platforms bound for St. Denys.

John Fairman

Noticeboard at Cowes.

John Fairman

The junction for the Netley route was St. Denys, 31816 crossing over from the Waterloo main line with a van train destined for Fratton.

E. Wilmshurst

Although not strictly within the administrative confines of Hampshire, no look at the railways of the county would be complete without a mention of the Isle of Wight system. The railways of the island were the province of elderly tank-engines and equally old stock which lasted in service until 1966. '02' 0-4-4 tank-engine 35, *Freshwater* shown at Cowes prior to departure for Newport and Ryde.

W. Gilburt

The first station out from Cowes was Mill Hill. The line passing through a narrow tunnel before entering the platform. Unfortunately, by 1964 the general appearance of much of the stock was poor although by comparison the stations retained much of their former glory, including as here capacious flower borders.

E. Wilmshurst

All the engines working on the island were named after island locations, No. 31, *Chale* crossing Cement Mills Viaduct on 19.2.66 with a Cowes bound train.

E. Wilmshurst

Today scenes such as this are but a memory, nearly all traces of the railway at Newport having been obliterated by commercial development. In happier times however, No. 28, *Ashey* crosses the River Medina swing bridge with a train for Ryde.

E. Wilmshurst

All that remains now of the railway system on the island is the short section between Ryde and Shanklin, the now preserved No. 24 *Calbourne* running south on this route shortly before the demise of steam.

A. Molyneaux

Despite the Southern railway sign, this was the approach to Ventnor well into BR days. The various fashions in both clothes and motor cars giving the whole scene a decidedly dated appearance.

Lens of Sutton

Back on the mainland another 0-4-4 tank-engine, this time 'M7', 30130 pauses at Hythe to take water on a Fawley service. This branch from Totton was one of the last railways to be built in the county not opening until 1925. Its late arrival on the scene recognised by the simple and basic design applied to the station buildings.

E. Wilmshurst

Besides Longmoor there existed another lesser known military line at Marchwood. Access on this occasion via the Fawley branch. It still survives, although operated by diesel traction. In 1958 however it was still steam worked, *Spyck* at the head of a single coach of London & South Western Railway origin.

Hugh Davies

Despite still being used for freight, views of trains on the Fawley branch are conspicuous by their absense, especially it would appear during the days of steam. On this occasion USA tank-engine, 30062 heads an RCTS special up the branch with Southampton water on the left and the heathland of the New Forest to the right.

W. Gilburt

The original route from Southampton to Dorchester ran through Ringwood and Wimborne, its sineous course earning it the nickname the 'Castlemans Corkscrew' after its main promoter a Mr Castleman. With the rise in popularity of Bournemouth during late Victorian times, it made sense to provide a more direct route from Brockenhurst via Sway. The Ringwood line immediately took second place with poorly patronised local services and consequently, short trains. One of these is shown here, 30109 at the head of a light two coach load at Holmesley in 1963. This section of railway now a motor road.

A. Molyneaux

Another cross country route passing through part of Hampshire was that from West Moors to Salisbury, a short section in the middle coming within the geographical limits of this book. As with so many lines it was a route for which the promoters had great hopes, these failing to materialise although their legacy in the form of underused facilities were apparent to the end. 76008 standing at Fordingbridge awaiting departure for Salisbury not long before passenger services were withdrawn in May 1964.

A. Molyneaux

Double headed engined trains were an unusual and seemingly rarely photographed feature of steam days although, here two have been recorded, both near Chandlers Ford and with trains of what appear to be pre-fabricated sections of track.

Both A. Molyneaux

Another 'M7', this time 30057 leaving Ringwood westwards and passing over one of several level crossings on the route. The station at Ringwood was unique for the type of covering applied to its footbridge. What appears to be an old bridge girder approached by wooden steps at either side with a corrugated iron roof and hardly providing any shelter to passengers.

T. Rowe

Before 1957 and the gradual introduction of diesel units on many of the local services these trains were steam hauled. The various combinations used were often an enthusiasts dream with a motley variety of locomotives and stock. A good example was photographed on a Romsey to Eastleigh local in 1952, ex LMS design 2-6-2 tank-engine, 41293 at the head of some LSWR coaches.
A. Molyneaux

In contrast here is one of the same services during the later diesel era, a three car 'Hampshire' diesel set about to leave Chandlers Ford station for Eastleigh, whilst in the distance a filthy diesel runs light in the opposite direction. Today the Chandlers Ford line has been singled and no longer has a regular passenger service, whilst the station and most of the associated buildings are demolished.
Hampshire Chronicle

East and west of Romsey were junctions leading to respectively, Redbridge and Andover. The latter remaining in use although the former 'Sprat & Winkle' line to Andover is long closed. Towards Andover its stations portrayed the characteristic charm of the rural railway, Horsebridge being a delightful example. The railway at this point was almost parallel with the renowned River Test.

E. Wilmshurst

The Romsey–Andover line was an unfortunate casualty of the diesel era. Its rural setting unable to generate sufficient traffic to warrant retention of the service. It had been hoped the diesel services would be saviour of such routes, although the one passenger at Fullerton Junction on 22.2.64 would hardly satisfy the accountants.

E. Wilmshurst

At Fullerton Junction another branch line made towards Wherwell, Longparish and Hurstbourne. Its course was through even more spartan countryside and so it was hardly surprising when passenger services were withdrawn in 1931. Goods however continued to run between Fullerton and Longparish for several years afterwards. 30289 in charge of this menial duty on 14.5.55.

Collection of Reg Randall

Cautiously leaving the up yard at Basingstoke, 34082, *615 Squadron* starts off with a train of containers. The engine possibly deputising for a failed 'S15'. Some drivers were not keen on the Pacifics at the head of freight services. Their likelyhood of slipping meant every start had to be made with extreme care.

Collection of Brian Davis

Besides the Bournemouth line trains, Basingstoke also saw a considerable number of services destined for Salisbury and the West Country. Many of these passing the station at speed. Unfortunately 35024, *East Asiatic Company* is prevented from doing so as it is switched from main to slow route through the station whilst working the down 'Atlantic Coast Express'. The cause being a broken rail and likely to result in a 5–6 minute delay.

Collection of Brian Davies

For a short tine during the 1950's the three S.R. diesels took it in turn to work certain of the principle express services, this including the 'A.C.E.' 10203 west of Basingstoke and unusually having received a caution aspect from the signal as it heads for Worting on 29.3.55.

Philip Kelley

An ideal spot for recording steam was at Worting Junction. 35023, by then un-named, pasing under the flyover with a Salisbury–Waterloo working. The presence of the M.A.S. signalling and electrified third rail an indication that the steam era was drawing to a close.

D. Mackinnon

Delays this time to one of the prestige passenger services. Unmodernised 'Merchant Navy', 35013, *Blue Funnel* on the 'Atlantic Coast Express' slowly passing over the viaduct.

British Railways

During the early part of 1951 work was carried out on the track bed of Hurstbourne Viaduct involving the injection of concrete below track level. Understandably there were heavy delays to traffic. An unidentified Drummond design cautiously approaching Hurstbourne station at the head of westbound goods.

British Railways

Other than the 'British Railways' on the tender, the livery of 30456 is little altered from Southern Railway days. Even the smoke deflectors still sporting their green livery. *Sir Galahad* depicted at Andover Junction station at the head of Maunsell coaching set No. 202.

R. Blencowe

Freight from Romsey having just joined the main line at Andover Junction. '700' class, 30368 at the head of two wagons of what appear to be sugar beet.

National Railway Museum, J.F. Russell Smith

Leaving Andover Junction for the Town station and Southampton via Romsey and Eastleigh. 30027 pulls away from the loop platform on its 1¼ hour journey.
National Railway Museum, J.F. Russell Smith.

Besides the main Southern line at Basingstoke, there was a north–south connection from the Western at Reading. The original layout having two stations alongside each other. This was the route used by many of the inter-regional trains running via Oxford. 6803, *Bucklebury Grange* just about to join the S.R. route with a parcels train for Southampton.
Collection of Brian Davis

From 1950 onwards control of the Basingstoke–Reading route was transferred to the S.R. although, until modernisation really took hold features from the old railway were commonplace. One of these was the signalling, the lever frame and gate wheel at Bramley in distinct Great Western styling.
British Railways

Still sadly missed today is the Winchester–Alton line, although part survives in the hands of a preservation society. The branch was also one of the first to be operated by diesel traction in 1957, with regular steam push–pull services withdrawn. Shortly before this the signalman at Winchester Junction collects the single line tablet from the fireman of 30130 as it joins the main line bound for Southampton Terminus.
Lens of Sutton

In contrast to the easy curves and gradients of the main line from Waterloo–Basingstoke, the Reading–Redhill route through north Hampshire was a switchback line abounding in restrictions and enough to test the capabilities of any engine and crew. Two cylinder 'Mogul' 31797 near Farnborough North with a train for Reading in April 1957.

Hugh Davies

During the lead up to full electrification the Mid-Hants line was also used a great deal as a diversionary route for Bournemouth line services. The only difficulty associated with this were the steep gradients on the branch which sometimes dictated double heading. Here a 'Mogul' has been attached ahead of the Merchant Navy working the 'Bournemouth Belle'. The pair seen approaching Alresford with the down service.

A. Molyneaux

Another special working, and pulling hard up the 1 in 60 of Medstead bank. The last active 'S15', 30837 at the head of an enthusiasts train. This particular tour was so popular it was repeated the following week.

A. Molyneaux

Finally on the Alton line, Medstead station and 34064 receiving assistance from 'D6556'. Unfortunately, the slipping characteristics of the 'Bulleid Pacifics' meant they were unreliable performers, the operating authorities obviously taking no chances especially in view of the wet conditions.

E. Wilmshurst

With the engine crew anxiously watching the man crossing the line ahead, an 'M7' tank-engine brings the Alton service into Droxford station on 2.2.55. Visible on the up platform are the canopy supports still in alternate black and white. This a throw back to the days of the black-out when station lighting was reduced and protruding objects highlighted as a means of assisting passengers.

Philip Kelley

The end in sight, literally, a Basingstoke service leaving Oakley shortly before both the end of steam and the closure of the station.

Hampshire Chronicle

Last rights on the Meon Valley, 31739 at Privett with the delightful sounding *West Meon Meteor* special. Closures in 1955 were still a relatively unusual feature although, even then some lines attracted more attention than others. Gosport for example closing with little ceremony whilst several trains ran to witness the last rights between Fareham and Alton.

W. Gilburt

At the south end of the line the Meon Valley made a connection into the Eastleigh–Fareham route at Knowle Junction before continuing south towards Fareham itself. 30718 bringing a Portsmouth train into the station although not one originating from the Meon Valley route.

National Railway Museum, P. Ransome Wallis

Alton station which apart from being the terminus of the Mid Hants route was also the limit of the electric service from Farnham. Both steam and elecric stock often then viewed side by side. On this occasion however, it is only one of the electric sets that is seen, the platform on the right without a conductor rail used for trains bound for Southampton.

Sean Bolan

First stop from Alton towards Fareham was at Farringdon Halt. The location seeing more in the way of goods than passengers. Just about to leave the small timber platform for Alton the extent of the yard is visible, the guard just in the process of giving the 'right-away' to his driver.
Philip Kelley

Bournemouth Central, 'a passing glimpse'.

Rod Hoyle